GOLF

WITH YOUR EYES SHUT

THE REVOLUTIONARY METHOD OF
BIRDY MULLIGAN

For permission requests, write to the publisher at the address below:
Reality Bites Publishing bv
Minervum 7444
4817 ZG Breda
The Netherlands
Saskia@realitybites.nu

Author: Birdy Mulligan
Redaction: Frank Wouters
Cover design: MIA
ISBN: 978-94-9078-360-0

© 2009-2023 Reality Bites Publishing bv

GOLF

WITH YOUR EYES SHUT

INTRODUCTION

My meeting with Birdy Mulligan changed my golf life. Until then, I naively walked my rounds and followed the path of trying, taking lessons, watching videos on YouTube, and navigating between hope and frustration. After my meeting with him, nothing was the same again on the golf course.

I had heard of him through a friend of mine who had played at Pinehurst in the United States. He told me the story he had heard from a fellow golfer of the mythical figure who went by the name of Birdy Mulligan. And so, I obsessively started to search for him to capture his remarkable story.

It was not easy to find him, let alone meet him in person. After several contacts via via we could see each other, for legal reasons in Canada, not far from the border with the U.S.A. The man did not take any chances. I had been thoroughly screened beforehand and afterwards I heard that he had been observing me for the 25 minutes he showed up late for the appointment.

The conversation in which he explained the principles of the book he was planning to write and the 9 holes we played during that time will always stay with me. Not only because we were playing for $1 a hole for fun, but he also gave me 10 strokes and I lost $8 in the end. His sober vision of golf and his irrefutable golf logic in particular made me think and – I admit – also doubt.

When I got back home and decided to follow his theory, I played my best round ever, playing about 7 strokes under my handicap in difficult circumstances. For the next year I could not keep this up until I got my hands on Birdy's manuscript, the book now before you. I read it in one sitting and my next game I played 5 points better than my level. I am far from scratch, but since then I no longer doubt Birdy Mulligan and his crazy theory, and I hope that after reading this book you will become as big a fan of him as I have become. Birdy Mulligan rules!

Frank Wouters
Publisher

A CONFESSION

You have probably never heard of me as a golfer, even though I have probably earned more money playing golf than most of the PGA pros you so admire. Tiger Woods and a few others may beat me, based purely on prize money, and you can probably add a few others to that list when you count endorsements. You do not know my nickname, Birdy Mulligan, and my real name probably will not mean much to you either, unless you've been unfortunate enough to run into me at one time or another.

I have made a lot of money and – sure – also lost a lot in the beginning because I was playing for money without having been listed as a pro. This is illegal, according to some people and in many legal systems around the world. Therefore, I cannot tell you my real name. There are even several layers built in between me and my publisher, because for most of the judges and public prosecutors in the places where I broke the gambling laws, the statute of limitations has not run out yet, even though I rarely play anymore and hardly ever for money these days. And according to my lawyer, even my first steps into the gambling circuit could still be considered as an ongoing misdemeanor, and this could cost me big time.

Yet, I still want to write this book. First, I am doing it because I do not think I have done anything wrong. I have trouble understanding what the difference is between the money Tiger Woods makes when he wins a competition and the money that I have earned. The only difference might be that my winnings come from my opponent. It may seem like I am trying to justify my actions, but when someone wins a professional tournament, this also happens at the expense of all the losers. Those who win, increase their market value, and can get more start money and endorsements, and those who lose, see their market value decrease. Same difference, I would say. Not only was I never allowed to receive any start monies or endorsements, but in this so-called free world, who gets to decide? I earned all my money – mostly honestly – by hitting a ball, not by showing up at the first hole in the latest Nike outfit.

Strictly speaking, I still have my amateur status, just like most of the people on the gambling circuit, and probably because you stand to lose more as a pro. If you get caught, you can never play golf again like everyone else, as a few of my colleagues have experienced in the Southwest.

Secondly, I want to write this book because an entire industry has developed around teaching golf and I am not sure whether I should laugh about it or get angry. Mastering the swing has become so complicated that I question whether this is really what it is all about. The more the game is taught, the less people seem to be able to play it properly. People used to start off with a handicap of 28 whereas a 36 is not even standard today anymore and you even hear of 45 and 54 being the norm nowadays. Yet it is not true that only talented people started playing golf in earlier times. On the contrary, my theory is that every sport that is favored by the so-called elite – snobs and people who are not used to working up a sweat – when it is clearly either easy, not tiring or both, at least not when played at a reasonable level. Just look at skiing, sailing or tennis, which in no manner or form can be compared to the technicality of pole vaulting or the degree of fatigue that accompanies the running of a marathon.

I am an outcast in the world of golf and yet I did not start playing golf any differently than you did. That is what this book is all about. Maybe I did get started a little differently, as the sale of the family business, a distributorship for Japanese car parts, made me a little wealthier than was good for me. With too much money and not really ready to grow up yet – I was 29 when I passed GO – I was still too restless to just be hitting balls. Now do not get too distracted by all of that, the point is I want to teach you how to play golf just like real golfers do, the gamblers who play for all the marbles. Not by the tiresome method that some spoon-fed pro in a polo shirt draped with an off-white sweater would teach you, but with a methodology from people who know that a single stroke could cost you

$1,000, $10,000 and at times even $100,000! If this is the feeling you want to learn and master, then read on.

I will not go into too much detail about the gambling circuit. I can understand that some of you might be curious, but I do not want to expose myself and quite honestly, I am not really that proud of what I have done, and I certainly wouldn't want to tempt any of you to go try it for yourselves. Maybe later... but for now, this is about something completely different. Let me take you back to a more innocent time, the time when I evolved from being a talentless loser to maybe the best gambling golfer in the world.

I am taking you with me because I am convinced that everyone, yes everyone, can attain the pro-level, as long your thought processes are organized and you start thinking like I do, as I was taught one fine day.

Yes, you read that right: in only one day!

-1-

Early in the 21st century on a golf course somewhere in the world

The difference between a mere low point and rock bottom is that the first one is still dynamic; something that at least shows some signs of life in it. A low point is a temporary phenomenon you just must get through. A little dip that you climb out of after a while and cool off, while rock bottom on the other hand leaves you out for the count without hope of ever getting up again.

Drama has always been inherent in the game of golf, and now I know why. The sun was shining, there was not a breath of wind and I was walking through magnificent surroundings. Normally this would fill a person's heart with happiness. Only I was playing golf and that for me was an impeding circumstance. Mentally I had bottomed out. I had decided to play a round on my home course after work and apparently, I was the only one who had this in mind. Which was just as well, because I would have felt even worse than I was then feeling about myself if someone had seen me messing around the way I was throughout the entire course.

Playing golf did not seem at all that difficult in the beginning. I was hitting quite a few balls straight and long. I seemed to have talent. It took me two attempts to get my golf license, which was not really that great, and that should have been a warning to me at the time. My mitigating circumstances were that the club rules were very strict and were enforced as such.

I started playing golf with a group of friends, rich friends. By chance we were lucky enough to have sold our companies just before the end of the previous millennium. The timing – just before the bursting of the Internet bubble – was not as critical for me as it was for John and Carl, who sold their web applications just in time. It was a little different for Dennis; he was an old friend with old money.

I will admit that I was spoiled, since I am third generation. Everything just simply fell into my lap, but after my Dad's death, I did not really feel obligated to carry on the family tradition anymore. I could have done it, but why would I go through the trouble of taking all that risk in a business not very close to my heart, when I could just cash in? So, this is how we wound up, with too much money and too much swagger, filling our days with things like endless lunches, travelling first class and playing golf for money. We would all start from scratch and started off by anteing $10 a hole, just for the fun of it. All of this was pleasantly disorganized and innocent at first, but the numbers quickly grew to $100 and $250 a hole as we became overconfident and started to challenge one another.

We could all leave the course relatively unscathed as all of us were pretty much even-steven, and even though a couple of thousand dollars was serious, it was something from which we could recover. What we did find out though, was that we were in a hurry to be good, because losing hurts, no matter what the number was.

I practiced a lot, without taking any lessons and that was not necessary either, as long as I could keep up with my friends. My game seemed to improve gradually this way. Nothing could stop me from becoming a decent player now.

That is when it started. The more I thought about playing with style and precision, the worse my results became. It was not just my score that was horrible, what was even worse is that even though I made my buffer most of the time, I just barely made it, which was why I wound up losing money on just about every game. They were not huge amounts, but still...

I counted on progressing quickly and with a calm and relaxed attitude, on gradually bringing my handicap down. Not that I played a lot of games using my handicap. That was not necessary when I was playing with my buddies. Instead of the gradual improvement I had hoped for, I wound up having to fight for every shot, and time and again I found myself in situations that you don't want to find yourself in: the ponds, the rough, the woods, everywhere except where I wanted to be.

It is really challenging when you get the feeling that your ball is allergic to the fairway. Golf starts to look more like a puzzle: how do I get out of the high grass? How do I get around that tree? Do I hit the ball out of that hazard, or do I take a penalty? After a while I became very skilled at getting myself out of trouble and managed to win quite a few holes that way. My opponents often thought I was lost and played too carefully, and my rescues took them off guard. It was exciting and frustrating at the same time, because I saw how others played a great hole, starting from the tee box over the fairway, onto the green and then putting the ball into the cup, done! Once in a while there would be a stroke too many, but they seemed to be more the small imperfections of an elegant dance rather than the cross-country competition I turned it into.

My first reaction was to take some lessons. I was convinced that the advice of a pro would definitely help me on my way to waking my sleeping talent. Even though the pro had a reputation of being more interested in female students, I had no problem ignoring this rumor. At the very least, you can expect a pro to live up to his name and reputation. Being a student like all others, I expected nothing less than a professional attitude. I remember the lesson like it was yesterday, no matter how hard I have tried to forget it.

Well, I was not disappointed when I showed up for that infamous first lesson.

"Grab your 7 iron," he started. I took the club he requested from my bag and assumed the starting position. The pro handily placed the ball in front of me on the practice mat and I was determined to give it a good, straight whack. I focused and at same time tried to relax. Feet perfectly positioned at shoulders' width, a nice loose grip with the v's between the thumb and hand pointing toward each shoulder and arms relaxed. Feet, hips and shoulders all lined up, hands just in front of the ball, head tilted slightly back and then in front of me, just above my right ear, a pitiful "Tsk, tsk, tsk!" Hmm, that last part did not belong in my routine.

I looked up and realized that the pitying sound was being produced by someone with experience, both in the game of golf and the enthusiastic rendering of that irritating sound.

"You've got the wrong club," the pro said. I looked at my club and turned the head around to check. It was in fact a 7 iron and I was puzzled.

"No, all of your clubs are wrong. You don't have the right set."

"I don't have the right set?" I repeated with a blank look.

I glanced over at my golf bag. Yup, it was mine all right. I will admit that they all looked alike, but I certainly was not mistaken.

"Nope, these are mine all right," I said sheepishly.

"Yeah, I get that, but they're not the right ones for you," the pro said, who was probably thinking that an IQ test might be a good idea when applying for a golf license.

Okay, I thought, I had bought a medium-priced set. Not exactly top of the line, but certainly a decent one at least.

"No matter, go ahead and finish your swing," said the pro, as if that was still possible.

I cleared my throat and repeated my routine. No more "tsks." This was a good sign for me to continue, so I slowly raised my outstretched arms and swung with a calm and natural movement through the ball. The light tap on the top of the ball seemed exactly what the ball had been waiting for to bounce off the tee and hobble off at an angle about thirty feet in front of me. In fact, so far to the right that it wound up in the tall grass at the edge of the driving range. In any case, the pro had convinced me that I really did need lessons.

It was then that I heard the second sound coming from the pro. "Tsk" was evidently used to point out the use of wrong clubs. Now it was a sound that came more from the side of the cheek and that sounded more like a "pshew." For a fleeting moment I thought that this might be a more positive message. Indeed, when I looked up, the pro was giving me a questionable look. I understood that the reason he did not start giving me advice right away was because of his good intentions. He needed some time to think about where he should start, and it took him some more time to figure out how to say this politely.

"Look," he said, "this is what you're doing." He eased me off the mat and took my club from my hands, while I shuffled over to a safe distance.

His stance did not seem that bad to me at all. If that were an imitation of what I had just done, I could live with that. He then swung and the ball hobbled the exact same way over towards the tall grass. It certainly was not his intention to ridicule me. He could have done a much better job of that. At least, that is what I thought a pro should be capable of, being that I had displayed new levels of ineptitude that had surpassed the stage of being laughable. But no, he was not exaggerating and the fact alone that he could duplicate my swing to a tee (no pun intended), was evidence enough of his ability.

"This is what you should be doing." He positioned himself in what appeared to be an identical stance again and produced what seemed to me, not only a smooth and perfect swing, but also one that resulted in perfect ball flight. This was amazing, only I had no idea what he was talking about.

"You get it?"

"Yup," I unexpectedly blurted out in complete support of my ego that had been completely sidetracked by my common sense.

"Great, try it again now."

I had myself to thank for that. I cleared my throat and calmly positioned my feet as if I had been doing this for years. In other words, I assumed my stance without really knowing what I should or should not have been doing. I still tried my darndest to imitate the pro's moves. I paid a little more attention to my stance, took a little more time on my grip and then started my swing. I did hit the ball this time but the outcome was disheartening. The ball shot off to the right against the board that separates the individual driving stations. The loud "crack" sound made everyone look over towards my station. I acted like nothing had happened so that my embarrassment could be limited to only the pro. At least he was getting paid to keep from laughing. He shook his head briefly and once again took my club from me. For a second there, his look made me feel like I might give him a contagious disease.

"I've got a nice set for you," he said casually, "but first look at this."

He teed up another ball, paused briefly and then produced

the perfect swing. The ball had a beautiful trajectory. I'd hit like that every now and then before, although I couldn't remember just how, and I had a funny feeling I wasn't going to learn anytime soon.

"Did you see that?"

"Did I see what?"

"My swing."

"Oh, of course, great!" I said correctly. "Superb. I wish I could do that."

"Okay, but did you learn something?"

"Yup, that I haven't a clue."

"That's not what I meant." I saw him swallowing a swearword. "Do you know what you're doing wrong now? Did you pay attention to what you need to do now?"

I clearly had no idea. What on earth should I be paying attention to? His feet, knees, hips, elbows, hands, head, stance, grip, posture, preparation, upswing, downswing, after-swing? Help! I suddenly got a rare dose of courage and decided to show my hand.

"Uh… no. I haven't a clue what to look for. Everything?" I tried timidly.

The pro sighed. "Right, you do need to pay attention to everything, but what I meant was the positioning of your wrists. You can probably make 37 mistakes in one swing."

He waited for these words to sink in and then consoled me by saying, "but you don't make all of them."

No, it just seems like this was my intention, I thought. That would have been much easier, as I was a lot closer to the 37 than I was to perfection. I figured, four more mistakes and I'll have made a complete idiot of myself.

"The most important thing at this point is your wrist. You bend it when you get at the top of your swing." He then proceeded to show it to me in perfect slow-motion and then I saw what he meant. Okay, no more than 32 potential mistakes to go. As soon as I get rid of those, everything will be perfect. Let us suppose I took weekly lessons dedicated to each mistake, practiced a little to perfect the new techniques, then my swing would be perfect in 32 weeks, as long as I didn't allow the mistakes to pile up. Then all I would need to do was learn how to putt, chip, pitch, take bunker shots, difficult lies ... Boy, I was suddenly feeling really depressed. I would never learn this game. Therefore, it did not come as a surprise that the lesson planned for the following week did not take place at all. Nevertheless, I had not made that decision at the time and surprisingly enough, neither had the pro.

I played John the week after the lesson and lost the largest amount of money ever. You could ask me exactly how much, but wasn't it Sigmund Freud who showed us how strong the human being is in suppressing our worst traumatic experiences? It was after that game that I knew he was right. This had nothing to do with the lesson, which had been fine, and the pro definitely knew what he was talking about, but what was just as clear was that I couldn't hit to save my life and I was worse off than ever before. It took all of my ability to concentrate just to focus on the proper positioning of my wrists and then suddenly I started to doubt everything.

I had two choices: the right one probably was to continue taking lessons and to gradually improve in that way, but I chose the other. My setback probably meant that I simply had to continue plodding on through the learning curve, the step you take backwards before you can take that leap forward. Still, I did not have the courage for that. I was probably living in denial, but that horrible game with John had robbed me of all my courage and self-confidence. The other choice was denial.

I initially went about playing leisure games by myself and only hit the course when it was quiet. This lasted for more than a month before I realized that I had regained my old lousy level of play. I swore I would never take another lesson for the rest of my life.

-2-

The game of golf is one helluva sport. I am convinced that the reason why so many people are so fascinated and sometimes even addicted to it is that you can never get it right. If that were all there was to it, there would not be any problem. You give it a try, it does not work for you, you quit. But this is what makes it a helluva game to play. In fact, you can never do it completely wrong either.

If I really thought that I had reached the bottom of the barrel and would never again recover, I'd have thrown my clubs into the pond a long time ago. Now I was relegated to just whacking some balls into it every once in a while and, what is even worse, without intent. Considering my skills, I had even come up short on that. Even though my body, brain, and my shrinking bank account – the stock market had crashed in the meantime – kept sending me signals that I had absolutely no talent for the game, something from the very depths of my heart kept telling me that I really could play and that it was just a matter of persevering. That voice was in fact the Golf Devil himself whispering his arguments in my ear, which were based on several empty statements of fact. Indeed, my play was poor in just about every aspect of the game, but this did not mean that there was no fertile ground wherein a seed of hope could grow. Every so often an amazing shot would miraculously come from my club. A swing that would suddenly catapult a ball straight as an arrow for a hundred and fifty yards with a sound that would bring back memories of the times when we used to make our own sounds symbolizing power and speed whilst swinging our swords made of cardboard. A twenty-foot putt that would follow the curvature of the grass, like an ice cube gliding over a woman's warm body only to wind up exactly where you want it to. A drive that would finally land way more than two hundred yards down on the middle of the fairway. An approach shot from eighty yards that would roll to a stop six inches from the hole. That is what makes it such a helluva game.

Something always keeps you on, or pulls you back onto the course, just like a gambler becomes addicted to gambling because he gets to win every now and then, just enough to believe that luck is on his side. Those are the two aspects of the game that came together for me. But playing golf has little to do with luck, even though you might start believing it sometimes. That is why I went out and bought sophisticated tees that I could adjust precisely to any height. I got me a hat because a cap seemed so lame to me. Everyone had a cap, but I was no Tiger Woods. I wanted my own style. Now with a hat, you stand out in a crowd and it helps to protect you from both the sun and the rain. Did I mention it helps you concentrate too? Yup, a hat is what it would be, with a wristband that had a little pouch for my marker that would also support my wrist and keep me from bending it.

I also bought a small device that could determine the ball's sweet spot. This would help me to tee up the ball facing in the right direction. Finally, as added assurance, I bought a lucky charm button shaped like a golf ball with the number 1 on it to pin on the brim of my hat. What could possibly go wrong now?

Well, as soon as it seems like you are "in the zone" and you think you have done all you could, including reaffirming your superstition, when you have hit a couple of nice strokes in a row and the ball does exactly what you wanted it to do, is exactly the time when destiny comes a-calling. Suddenly things start going wrong and you slice that beautiful drive you plonked down the middle of the fairway right into the woods with your second shot. You chip the straight-as-an-arrow ball way too hard left into the pond behind the green. You inexplicably miss the straight six-inch putt following that beautiful eighty-yard approach shot you just made. The latter happened to me on the 18th hole that day and it was a return to reality, just like the shadow of a raincloud that had hung over all the other holes. I could not play the game and probably would not ever be able to either. If I were to get any better at this game, it would have to be bit by bit. It would mean that I would have to erase every mistake, one by one. I would have to start taking lessons again.

I started to get depressed thinking about the long road ahead of me. A road that only my spirit and the perseverance of taking lessons week after week would enable me to catch up to the head start that others had on me because of their talent. Meanwhile this was starting to cost me money, as my friends had now raised the stakes to an average of $500 a hole. I didn't want to be left behind and was quietly becoming desperate, since my stock had taken quite a beating, and this meant I couldn't live from the dividends anymore. The situation was even worse for John because his company's takeover was largely paid for with shares from another Internet company.

The desperation as a result of my poor game, the urge to want to continue playing for money and my financial situation had me desperately searching.

Could it be that a short cut still existed somewhere? Was there something about the essence of the game that I was not getting? Maybe I was making just one basic mistake? Just imagine that, it seemed impossible. One of my buddies had told me that your swing only starts to settle down once you have hit 10,000 balls. I was not even close to that yet, although I kind of thought I had already lost as many. Friends, family and acquaintances gave me golf balls on every holiday and all my birthdays. I was quick in deciding not to get too emotionally attached to this, as it would take me only three holes before I lost the first one in a pond that without a doubt would have a "No Fishing" sign posted. I was just considering taking up fishing to relax. I would then buy me a pond and post a sign that read "No Golfing."

-3-

"You know the whole idea behind playing golf is that you should relax," Maria said that night at the dinner table. She managed to sum up in one sentence the essence of everything I had still not accomplished. She was right. The round I had played that day did nothing but frustrate me. That was not the ideal way to spend your leisure time. But on the other hand, learning something is always less fun than being able to do something. If this were something temporary, I would still have to persevere and try to learn from my mistakes. My wife did not know I was playing for money and that I was losing an average of $4,000 a week.

I ate my dinner in silence and have to admit I wasn't very good company. I was so inwardly focused that I was barely aware of my surroundings. It was as if there was something else to my performance, which Winston Churchill had expressed as a perfect stroll ruined by hitting a little white ball with instruments that are in no way suitable. The only problem being that

I was losing an average of $2,000 a stroll with it.

"Oh, by the way, those books on golf you ordered just came in the mail," said Maria.

That is right; those were the books I had ordered to do some home studying in my spare time. Having been a former student, I figured this would work for me. If I could review the steps I had to undertake one by one with photos and explanations by famous golfers, I would be able to absorb the minute details of the game, away from all the pressure.

"They're on your desk."

"Thanks, love," I mumbled. She had left the table and nestled herself on the couch in front of the TV and I headed over to my desk.

I looked at the package, sighed, grabbed a pair of scissors, and cut the string. I made a clumsy effort to undo the wrapping. The tape was very resilient, and I could not get my fingers under it properly since as of late I had been keeping my nails short. I grabbed the scissors again and snipped at the wrapping.

Four books appeared to me as if emerging from an egg. Two were green, one yellow and the fourth was a somewhat larger book with a blue, hard cover. I took hold of the last book, the blue one. It was pretty thick. 240 large-scale pages should be able to make it clear to me how I should use a metal club to hit a little ball made of undetermined materials into a hole in the grass. 240 pages probably full of photos.

I was not surprised I could not play. Whose brain could capture this? Certainly not mine. Nevertheless, I got comfortable in my reading chair and started to leaf though the book.

Every page was a rollercoaster of emotions ranging between hope and desperation. I discovered on page 17, just after the Table of Contents, the Preface and the Introduction, then again on page 18 and 19 and then twice on page 25, what I had been doing wrong. I decided to stop before the abundance of information sent my brain into overload, and started to apply the first newly-learned principles on the very next day.

-4-

It was 7 o'clock in the morning and dew still covered the grass when, with my newfound confidence, I once again stepped onto the course. The clubhouse was still shut. The green keeper had opened the door at 6.45 a.m. When I arrived, I just happened to see him heading for his toolshed. I calmly unloaded my golf bag and walked with my head held high towards the first tee. I was now going to practically apply the first 25 pages of my recently-purchased 240-page book. This did not cover much more than grip and stance, but I had to start somewhere.

I carefully removed my 7 iron from the bag so as not to go overboard on the 265-yard dogleg par 4. I carefully placed the ball on the tee I had just planted as if it were a diamond in a showcase on New York's 5th Avenue. I avoided placing the tee too high so as to be able to make the required distance and land in the corner. I took hold of the club in the manner described in the book in an almost ritual fashion, checked my grip again and got into my stance. I estimated the direction the ball needed to go for it to land right in the middle of the fairway in the direction of the flag. The pond 30 yards in front of me should not be a problem. I took my stance, took another look at the spot where I wanted the ball to land and calmly started on my swing. A little bit of height would be just enough to ensure a nice flight of at least 130 yards with a roll-out of about 10 yards or so, maybe just a bit more because of the dew. There was a light breeze from left to right, but not enough to have to consider it in relation to the broad fairway ahead of me, especially since I was not counting on hitting the ball too high. My backswing peaked and with a masterly stroke, I planted my club straight into the ground. It was the sod that pushed the ball forward, whereupon it proceeded to roll 10 yards at an exasperatingly slow pace right into the pond. I sighed deeply.

Walking those 10 yards to drop a ball over there seemed senseless to me at this point. No, even worse yet, this was way below my dignity. I decided to start anew from the tee.

Take two deep breaths, concentrate again and repeat the routine. Everything was looking good up until then, as with the hole I had furrowed around my tee, it was highly unlikely that that I would excavate any more sod this time. An identical stroke would now land perfectly under the ball and send it off on its originally-planned trajectory. I routinely swung and hit the top of the ball, which sent it off in the same direction once again, albeit now in a different manner. The only progress was that the second ball made it to the pond faster. I'm not sure whether I was more desperate than frustrated, or maybe even angry... how about furious? I could just barely resist tossing the club with all my might right after the ball into the pond. How I hated this sport, this game, this hellish pastime, this devilish hobby! How was it humanly possible that I was capable of producing the exact same result in two different ways, while there are gifted people on this earth who can probably do it properly in five different ways?

I sat down on the elevated tee area to consider my options. Stopping was the first thing that came to my mind. It started to dawn on me that the high registration fees were all part of a brilliant, malicious and worldwide conspiracy called golf, and once you've paid all this money, you couldn't quit just like that. Accepting defeat is always difficult, especially when it comes down to only you. Yet I continued to believe in my newfound form of autodidactic learning. It was too early to abandon the course. The desired results might not be mine yet, but then again, I had only gotten to page 25 so far. I did nothing but sigh and look around for about ten minutes. I had calmed down a bit. I planned to finish off a couple of holes and then head back home to study.

I played reasonably well on the remaining holes. I chalked up some points here and there, but as soon as I got the feeling that I was making progress, I started hitting balls every which way. Only my putting seemed to go relatively well. Unfortunately, the ball must preferably be on the green in order to putt, and this was rarely the case. Maybe I should take up miniature golf instead… costs less. I am sure I could find some kid who would play me for 10 cents a hole.

I never got close to a golf course over the following weeks, at least not a real one. I'd seen them all in photos, because every evening I devoured the knowledge that the famous golf pros from around the world had poured into my books, richly illustrated with examples and pictures of real-life situations. I avoided my golf buddies who were taking turns calling me. They had started playing with others from the gambling circuit in the meantime and even they got their clocks cleaned. How Carl managed to survive that was a mystery to me. I was dead set on not getting involved with that for now, although they seemed to enjoy it. Maybe they wanted to drag me down with them. They did send me a message together with a phone number for "the Broker."

"The Broker" is a shifty character whose phone number changes every month, who brings golf gamblers together. He decides how many strokes either you or your opponent gets. He sort of elects himself to be the handicap commission in this way. Don't ask me how he does it, but his judgment usually turns out to be amazingly sharp and on the ball. He earns 1% of the total inlay in a contest and he is out for good if he screws someone or does not get the percentages right. You can use him to challenge a particular player, send a general call-out or simply have him call you.

If you ask me why I continued playing for money later on, it was because the feeling that you were going to be called was probably the most exciting feeling I'd ever experienced in my life. Time and time again it gave you that feeling of tension that can only be compared to moments in your adolescence when you are crazy in love with a girl and you are not sure whether the feeling is mutual, but you decide to go for it. The competition that ensues after the call is like your first date and it is that moment, that feeling you experience again and again, no matter how many times you do it. Nevertheless, even though I can sympathize with your curiosity, I would prefer not to go any further into the betting aspects of the game.

In my mind I started to get better and better. I started to have a better understanding of the instructions that the pro had given me during my one and only lesson, in the sense that I could now place them in the bigger picture. I was not only struggling through the 240 pages of the first book. The other books were also the subject of my undivided attention, supplemented by four DVDs and tips from pros I had found on the Internet. I was a walking encyclopedia. I had once heard of an East-German swimming coach who had been tremendously successful without ever having swum a single stroke. I was convinced that I had become a good golfer without ever having hit a single ball.

In all my optimism – we were now two months further – I decided to call the Broker. We spoke briefly, with him mainly inquiring about my references. He said that as a new customer he assessed me a bit cautiously. It was only after he hung up that I started to reflect on what he had actually meant by that: cautious for me or for him? Luckily enough the game turned out to be a so-called low-inlay-game. That meant $1,000 a hole. I had done that before and the most I could lose was $18,000.

I took that number into consideration so that in my mind every hole meant a profit of $1,000. A draw on a hole paid $500. This setup could be fun. Do not for one moment think that I was such a good golfer at the time or that it was only the ace players who did the gambling.

My handicap might have even been over 30 at that point in time. I was just like any other player in the beginning; I had the urge to play for money and trusted that the event would be a fair one. The latter, by the way, applies more to gamblers than it does to amateurs. Maybe because more people are watching you and you never really know whether or not your opponent or the broker is really linked to the Mafia.

-5-

I did not really behave like a real sportsman on the night before my first competition against an unknown opponent. Rather more like someone who had just celebrated an important victory. That was certainly a little presumptuous of me, but I wanted to get it over and done with. Luckily enough, arrogance comes before a fall, since it is absolutely worthless to you afterwards. And on top of that, you seem foolish.

My head and arms were heavy during the competition on the next day under conditions that I cannot remember clearly anymore.

Strangely enough, I played a decent round and managed somehow or another to win $1,000. That and the endless respect of my buddies was the reward for all my hard theoretical work. I now questioned whether practice was necessary at all. Despite all the disdain I had experienced during the past weeks in the clubhouse, I had evidently unconsciously put my study to work and every now and then something unexplainable would show up in my game. This was probably because I had gone over the routines countless times in my mind. I decided not to think about it anymore and just to enjoy it. I had only myself and my study methods to thank for this. I had now sworn off my superstitions and was now completely relegated to knowledge... well, maybe not completely.

Specifically, I had come to the conclusion that my equipment had been the crux of my inexplicable failing. I had begged the pro to tell me more about the golf set he had mentioned after giving me my one lesson on that fateful day. He was very professional about it and I sensed no malicious intent. He had carefully analyzed my swing and in fact, the set was the second item I wound up having to cough up money for in my short golfing career, though it was not all that expensive.

"The expensive set would come as I started to play a little better and my handicap dropped to below 15 or so," said the pro.

That then, was my financial windfall for the future, since the point where I was to improve significantly seemed, despite my reasonable round, not to be happening anytime soon. The pro did not know that I was not playing with an official handicap anymore, but for cash. I felt I was very much like the pro, only I was undercover and had poor skills. I really could not play the game that well at all.

I bought the most expensive pair of gloves I could find to go along with the set. I also invested in a pair of shoes that would make the average PGA-tour player green with envy, and with this and with all the new stuff, a new me was born, except for my putter, since that was working well for me. I looked great on the course and that alone gave me a boost of self-confidence. Maybe one's equipment was that important after all and my good score on that day I attributed to that.

That moment of glory was motivating enough to get me out onto the course the very next day at sunrise. I can be brief here: I played reasonably well but did not quite make the buffer for my fictitious handicap (25). In other words, I allowed myself to flub the first hole, did not count the missed putt on the third, or the air swing (I know!) on the fifth. They say that your handicap reflects the number of hours you work a week. I would have to find a part-time job to match mine. Boy, was I kidding myself or what. It was clear to me – my dream of becoming a good or at least above-average player was smothered under a lack of talent, which I would pass off to my friends as being a lack of time.

The latter I would make believable by not touching a club for a month. In any case, this hiatus would give me the time to heal my frustrations and repair the dent in my ego.

-6-

My busy schedule made it very easy for me to keep my word. I actually didn't touch a club for a period of two months, mainly because fate decided to intervene, every time I was tempted to drag myself out to the course, by making it rain. Under those circumstances, it did not take much to convince me to stay indoors. It did not even have to be a downpour; a little drizzle was largely sufficient. After a while, fate took such a hold of me that even an overcast sky did the trick. I systematically refused invitations to go play golf with friends or former business acquaintances by not finding any free time anywhere in my schedule.

It was Maria, of course, who asked me why I had not been playing golf recently. She knew that I was involved in putting some deals together here and there to make some extra cash but was also familiar with my ability to find some free time when I really needed it. Was it time to confess to her that I had no talent for the game? I am sure she was already well aware of it as she knows me like no one else, but the fact that I would have to admit it to myself was something completely different.

"You hardly play with Dennis anymore," she said to me one evening.

I knew why I was not playing with Dennis anymore. "Oh yeah, Dennis... Well, would you like to play with someone who always starts gabbing right when you want to tee off? Or with someone who walks through your putting line? Or with someone who clearly has no respect for etiquette and even ridicules you when you're struggling?"

"No, I wouldn't like that at all," Maria responded.

"Well, neither does Dennis."

Ha-ha! At least golf could still make me laugh every now and then. This was a nice way to suppress my frustrations, as playing poorly and not making any progress was so frustrating, considering all the money I was losing. I had heard that joke during my last competition and for two months now I'd been itching to use it again on someone else. "Honey, ..."

"I'm going to play again, really. It's just a matter of... time, concentration, feeling like it and the weather. It's never the right weather. It'll come. Maybe I'll go tomorrow or the day after, not one day later."

Inwardly I was scared, as things can really speed up at $1,000 a hole. In the eyes of the average working man, I might still have a small fortune sitting in my bank account. The problem was that I had once started with a big fortune.

It took a week before I realized that I was wasting my nights away in front of the TV, that I had not tasted the smell of fresh air in more than a month and that it might be time to start following a ball around again. My new set of clubs had gradually slipped to the back of my garage. Not consciously, mind you, it is simply because everything in our garage always retreats towards the back and is unjustly buried under all the newer stuff. At one point even the effort it would take me to go furrow my golf bag out from the depths of the garage became a reason to drag myself back in front of the TV, but after a while I managed to discipline myself. The weather was acceptable but cloudy, with a bit of a breeze at the end of a beautiful summer day and when our golf course is traditionally as good as deserted in the evenings.

I took a deep breath at the first tee and tried to free my spirit from all its stored knowledge. My first couple of strokes went well. I seemed to have forgotten what I did wrong, but by the fourth hole I was quick to fall back into my old mistakes again. The wind became more and more bothersome and before long it looked like I was in for a torrential downpour. I could smell the rain approaching in the distance.

I was overtaken by a man of similar age at the third hole, who appeared to be in a hurry to finish his round. He was quite a bit shorter than me, muscular and somewhat sinewy. He was waiting at the tee of the next hole while I was desperately trying to reach the green with my second stroke on a par 3. I signaled him that he could tee off, hoping that I would get rid of him quickly. He was not showing any signs of becoming impatient, but I was embarrassed by my ineptitude. He casually hit the ball, which took flight with an elegant curve, landed on the green and then continued to roll a bit, only to have the backspin pull it back some three feet from the hole. I sighed deeply. I would like to be able to play like that, but it was clear that this was not on the cards for me. Sure, every now and then with a lucky shot, and most of the time when nobody was looking. Obviously, all of this could be perfectly explained statistically.

In the meantime, the man had reached the green and I managed to get my ball there as well. With a gracious effort I gestured as if I was making the green available to him. I removed the flag from the hole, and he birdied it. I laid down the flag and proceeded to putt. Wow… that one dropped in nicely! Putting was not my problem.

"You want to walk together?" he asked casually.

This was exactly what I did not want to hear as I did not need an audience to witness my bungling. Maybe I could learn something from his style, although I was not looking forward to any kind of criticism, as it would only be the umpteenth piece of advice that would further confuse me. "I don't want to hold you up," I said, in all sincerity.

"It doesn't really matter to me. I don't mind a little bit of company, otherwise it's often nothing more than just walking and hitting a ball. I rarely play."

Oh, how I abhorred the arrogance of these people who supposedly hardly ever play and yet seem to burst at the seams with talent. You run into them often enough, although not on the golf course most of the time, so you could never prove that they were just showing off. I probably just had a distinct loathing for my own lack of talent and was confusing my disdain with jealousy.

"Play a lot?" he asked.

"Not often, but a lot," I sort of mumbled in response.

He looked at me quizzically.

"What I meant was, I don't come to the course that much, but once I'm here, I hit a lot of balls before I'm done."

"Oh, like that." A slight smile appeared on his face.

We both pulled our trolleys to the next hole. The clouds continued to gather ever so menacingly over the course as if they were preparing to inundate the fairway.

"Why are you having such a hard time?" he asked me, still smiling.

Oh boy, here it came. I'd have to explain my miserable situation all over again.

He pulled out his driver and teed up his ball for a long par 4. Without hesitation and with a mighty swing, he planted his club on the ball and instantly propelled it into majestic flight, only for it to land 280 yards further down on the fairway.

I swallowed. "Uh, I gave it all I had." I too, grabbed my driver. It seemed a bit ridiculous at that moment to go through my complicated pre-shot routine, only to flub my shot. Maybe I should have been just as blasé as he was. I teed up and gave the ball a whack. The shot was not as bad as I had become accustomed to recently. Okay, I had put quite a bit of slice on the ball, but the field-sized fairway ahead of me saved me from being penalized with an out-of-bounds.

"Not too much of a problem," he said, comfortingly.

"I'm not doing too badly right now, but honestly, I'm terrible. What's your handicap?"

"I'm a pro."

"Okay, that explains a lot. I don't have that ambition," I lied.

"You don't need to be a pro to play well and have fun."

"Have you been a pro for long?"

"For quite a few years now."

He seemed to be a man of few words. Normally, I would have liked that. Although certain people consider golf to be a social activity, I considered it to be an excellent example of an individual sport. I still wanted to know more.

I had arrived at my ball and botched my next shot. To avoid attracting too much attention to my game, I decided to ask some more questions. "How long did it take you to become a pro? Was it something you dreamed off since you were a small boy?"

"No, I sort of fell into it. It actually happened pretty coincidentally."

"Oh, you woke up one day and suddenly you were a pro?"

"Nope, it wasn't like that. I woke up and suddenly I was a pro's assistant."

"I woke up this morning and I still couldn't play golf."

He laughed. "I was actually an entertainer at a vacation resort and one day the pro needed an assistant. There wasn't anybody around who could play golf, but I just happened to be available that day, so they sent me. It could just as well have been for archery."

"That's when you started loving it?"

"No, not really, but since I was going to be the assistant for quite a while, I figured I might as well learn the game."

"So, you had never played before?"

"Never held a club in my hands."

"Well, how did it go?"

"It had to. The pro wasn't always there, and I had to figure out quickly how I was going to teach the guests."

"That must have been hilarious!"

"Yup, it was pretty weird. Luckily enough, most of the vacationers were regulars and not diehard golfers. That gave me a bit of time."

"Did you have talent?"

"Maybe, but I think more importantly, I quickly developed a method. Or should I say, I met someone and then I had a method."

We arrived where my ball was. I grabbed my 8 iron and took my stance, glanced briefly at the flag and swung. I drove the head of my club into the ground. Not straight in, the ball had a bit of flight to it, but not much more than 60 yards.

"Hmm..." the pro said.

"Speaking of encounters, allow me to introduce myself." I said in a vain attempt to avoid my blooper getting once again too much attention. "Mulligan, Bogey Mulligan[1]."

"Coach."

It was just at then that the impending rainstorm broke loose in all its summer intensity. We looked at each other as if to ask what we needed to do. I was not the type to run and hide from a couple of spatters. They say it never rains on a golf course,

don't they?

On the other hand, playing poorly was not much fun either, let alone in the rain. I saw the same thought in Coach's eyes. Luckily enough, we were saved by a bolt of lightning that for an instant, lit up the dark sky caused by the rain, followed by an amazing thunderclap. There was no room for doubt now;

1 This is what my golf buddies called me at the time. Actually, they called me Double Bogey Mulligan, but I certainly wasn't going to introduce myself as such.

we needed to get off the course. Swinging a metal club above your head in an open field during a rainstorm is never a good idea and was reason enough for us to quit playing. It's weird how everything seems to be arranged in golf, even when to stop or continue. We left our balls behind and high-tailed it back to the shelter.

We were soaking wet before completing that hundred-yard dash. We sat down on the bench and I was panting much more than he was. We watched silently as this phenomenon of nature developed around us.

"So, you had a method after this encounter?" I said, breaking the silence.

"Yes, I met a man who was quick to set me on the right track. He is more of a guru than a golfer."

"Sounds kind of heavy. But anybody can call himself a guru nowadays," I said somewhat indifferently.

"That's true," he agreed, "but this man is truly amazing. An encounter with him will change your golf life."

"Is he a well-known golfer?"

"No, you don't know him. He doesn't play competitions. I was his first pupil, just briefly. Everyone tried to discourage me from doing it, even thought I was nuts, but I wanted to turn pro quickly."

"And it worked? How long was it before you turned pro?" I asked.

"I had a 5 handicap within a year and a half."

"Five? As in 1, 2, 3, 4, 5? Wow!"

"And 6 months later I got my PGA-license."

"Boy, I wish I had that talent."

"It's not a matter of talent," he gently countered.

"Of course it is."

"You know, I always hear the same old story, but I'm not super-talented and nothing special physically. Naturally, I was playing golf on a daily basis, but the rest is pretty simple."

A snuffling laugh escaped me as I thought of my shoddy play. "That's some passion you must've had!"

"It had nothing to do with passion for me personally. You need to know that I've never played the game as if it were my hobby. For me, it was a skill not unlike what the bricklayer would require to lay bricks and build a wall."

The rain started coming down harder on the roof of the shelter and we gradually started talking louder.

"Okay, what's the secret?" I almost shouted.

Coach glanced at his watch. "Wow, is it that late already?" That seemed like a pretty obvious ploy to get rid of me.

"No, Coach, you can't do this to me – leave me hanging like that."

"I'm sorry, I really have to go. I was only playing a couple of holes because a student of mine cancelled at the last minute."

I placed my arm on his and looked at him. He smiled. It seemed like the thunder was passing us by.

"Okay, I'll give you the basics." He cleared his throat. "And that starts with a generally-known basic principle about the essence of the game of golf: contrary to other sports like tennis and football, golf is a sport that revolves around not making mistakes. It may be enough in other sports to exhibit a few flashes of genius in order to win a competition." A rolling thunder added drama to his words.

"That's impossible in golf: an outstanding play makes no

sense if you make any mistakes before or after it. The winner of the competition is the man or woman who makes the least number of mistakes. Look at the basketball player who misses half of his shots. He can throw the ball fifty times during a game, but he is only hailed as the MVP if he throws the winning three-pointer at the buzzer. A soccer player, bicycle racer or tennis player can often decide the outcome of a competition by executing an outstanding play. Do you remember Ronaldo, the Brazilian soccer player? It often seemed like he was just dragging his feet on the field for 89 minutes, only to decide the outcome of the match in the last minute with a never-before-seen outstanding play. You can limit yourself in tennis to hitting perfect returns only, but you need to hope your opponent makes a mistake. The best of tennis players take control of the match and hit brilliantly-placed winners to force their opponents into impossible situations. Even in chess you can tell the way in which real talent distinguishes itself from the average chess player. The average chess player hopes that the opponent will make a mistake. The grandmaster develops a personal winning strategy."

"And in golf?"

"Most of those at the beginner level hope for that impossible shot that will make their day, but it's really nothing but mere consolation for inconsistent play."

I knew exactly what he was talking about. "And so?"

"Golf is about not making mistakes. He who makes no mistakes is perfect. Compensating for mistakes by making outstanding plays are the straws that beginners clutch onto. Obviously, pros seem to succeed in doing that from time to time, but they've already suffered defeat at that point. Even the soccer player who doesn't make a mistake plays an average-to-good match, depending on the play of the opposing team. A golfer who makes no mistakes plays a world-class competition, no matter what the competition's results are."

I had already pulled a business card from my golf bag. "Okay, I got that."

"Then here's the next basic principle. Execution in the game of golf is not difficult at all. Every mistake you make is rooted in a fallacy, a wrong swing thought."

"A mental error, you mean? Well, once, while I was hesitating at the tee, a friend of mine yelled: "This isn't a mind game, you know!""

Coach smiled. "But it is. Poor execution of a stroke is the result of a mental error."

"Wow, that's really heavy. I can hardly believe it's really like that."

"Maybe that's your first mental error."

"Okay, that's smart, but be more precise and give me an example."

Coach glanced at his watch again.

"Okay, but let's keep it simple, because the game of golf is simple."

Yeah, simple for you, I thought.

"What's your biggest problem?"

I thought for a while, not because I could not think of a problem, but because I had so many to choose from.

"I hit the turf quite often and it's not just annoying. Sometimes after a game my forearms really hurt."

Coach smiled at me briefly but did not seem sympathetic. "Well, that's because of a mental error."

I nodded cynically. "That doesn't surprise me. According to you, every mistake is a mental error."

He laughed out loud.

I glanced ahead of me for an instant and noticed that the worst of the rainstorm had passed. "And which mental error do I make then?" I continued.

"What part of the ball do you want to hit?"

I thought about it and hesitated. I had never given it any thought. "The underside, I want to get nicely under the ball so I can launch it up high."

"That is your fallacy."

"What do you mean?"

"You can try and hit the ball in many different spots, but there is one spot you can't hit."

"The inside?"

Coach started to laugh.

"Yes, you're right. Okay, then: there's a part of the outside of the ball that you can't hit."

I raised my eyebrows as it suddenly became clear to me. "Of course... the underside."

"That's right, because that side is on the ground. Your efforts to hit the impossible side, is causing you to hit the ground."

He once again hastily looked at his watch and stood up. In the meantime, breaks had appeared in the rainclouds and the rainstorm had cried itself out to only a few remaining tears.

"But wait a minute," I continued. "I sometimes also hit the top of the ball. What's the mental error there?"

"It's the same one, only you added an additional aspect to it. You still want to hit the bottom of the ball, but at the same time, you don't want to hit the ground."

"That's right."

"Therefore, you go through all the motions to get under the ball but pull up just before contact. Topping is unavoidable then."

Coach shook my hand. I gave him my business card and he took off running.

"But what I am I supposed to do?" I yelled after him.

He turned to look at me while continuing to run. "Hit the ball!"

"What?"

"It's simple, don't think about anything and just hit the ball!" I saw him pick up his ball in the distance and then disappear.

Hitting the ball? Was that the advice of a pro? What was that all about? I remained seated for a while, not so much to wait until it was completely dry, but more because I wanted to think some more about what Coach had said. Maybe even more about the doubts I had as to whether or not he had been sincere, or if he had just been pulling my leg.

I stood up with a sigh and decided to walk over to my ball. I had no desire to head over to the next tee. I was more confused than ever. Deep in my thoughts, I kept on walking a bit and then dropped my ball on the fairway that leads towards the clubhouse. I took my stance and casually hit the ball using a 7 iron and sure enough, the ball took off straight and flew for a good distance. Not my usual distance, but close to it. Hmm, maybe, just maybe...

It was a par 5 hole, so I had a long way to go yet. I stayed with the 7 iron so as not to lose my confidence. Once again, I just hit the ball. It took off straight as an arrow again. I was about 100 yards from the green now. Could it really be true? I took out my sand wedge to bridge the last 100 yards. I spent a little more time on my stance this time around, swung and with a nice arc, the ball floated to a point about 20 yards left of the outer edge of the green, right on the tee box of the following hole.

Too bad, there goes my perfect streak. So, the wonder that seemed to be revealing itself to me was not to be.

It was getting late. I picked up my ball and decided to call it a day.

-7-

A spark of confidence must have been ignited after my conversation with Coach because I signed up for a stroke play competition at the club the next weekend as a regular player. My goal was to adjust my handicap and show my stuff at the club at the same time. Apart from my love-hate relationship with golf, I needed to start playing competitions sooner or later; otherwise, I still would not have a good indication of my level of play. Regardless, whether you play for money or not, you cannot demand any respect if you are not competing and do not have a decent handicap.

You then belong to the players who have tossed the rulebook into the ring and under the ruse of playing recreationally, have actually given up on ever getting any better. I was not there yet, not by a long shot. I had found new hope. But hope provides no assurances. I was sure it could not be as easy as Coach had explained, but I decided to stick with his instructions anyway. This, against my better judgment, was just to prove him wrong. He was just a very gifted player. Those people always think that what they do is so very simple and are consequently amazed when the average Joe cannot do it.

I experienced something in the days preceding the competition that reinforced the theory that Coach had shared with me. I was invited by a friend of mine to play some golf on his club's prestigious course. He did not usually play for money. As the reserved tee time was rather late in the day, we questioned whether we would make it back to the clubhouse before nightfall. My friend had told me on the phone that I should not worry as the course really had not been particularly busy, and we could play at a brisk pace. Apparently for many, having membership was a matter of prestige rather than an opportunity to play golf frequently.

After 4 p.m. they even stopped taking reservations for tee times. You could start whenever you wanted to. I had just pulled into the parking lot when I received a phone call. My playing partner informed me that he was going to be pretty late, something about unexpected problems at work. We decided to meet at the driving range and as he was late, he suggested to my amazement that we play for $100 a hole. I have never warmed up as I had on that day, since my buddy showed up almost an hour late and then wanted to hit some balls himself. Due to my poor physical condition, my expiration date was long gone by that time.

The result was a very moderate start at the first hole, followed by a series of inconsistent shots that had me lingering on the verge of frustration. Other than that, it was an enjoyable game, even if I was $300 in the hole, but a remarkable incident that happened on the 18th hole reminded me of what Coach had said. Even though the course was indeed quiet, we did not succeed in getting back before dark. We were at the last hole, a par 4 that we had to finish in the waning hours of daylight. We could barely see the white flag up ahead at about 347 yards, which seemed to have morphed into a bluish color from the nearby interior lighting of the clubhouse. We decided to play one more hole just for fun, even though we knew that every ball that did not land on the fairway would be hopelessly lost.

Considering the quality of my game at the time, that would only take one stroke, I thought. I also suggested we do double or nothing on that last hole. Whether I lost $300 or $600 did not seem to make much difference.

Against all odds, we produced shots that seemed magnificent to both of us. Only there was no way of knowing this for sure, since it was impossible to follow the ball, but we had already conceded to that before teeing off. That is why we were having so much fun, just like kids waiting to see what Santa had left under the Christmas tree for them. We strolled further down the fairway and found our balls close together near the yellow disk, no more than 4 yards apart at about 150 yards from the edge of the green.

We once again hit our balls blindly in the direction we thought the flag to be. The sound of the ball hitting metal was clear, almost like the tap on a crystal glass. We pulled our caddies further towards the green, hoping that we had estimated the distance to the green correctly and had not messed up on the direction. If this were not the case, we would still have behaved as a pair of mischievous and reckless young boys, who thought that they could play in the dark. We could hardly control our happiness upon arriving at the green. We fell about the place as we neared the flag. My buddy's ball was about 3 yards from the hole and mine was positioned at less than 2 feet. He still needed two putts and I came close to missing my birdie since emotions of amazement and joy were clouding my ability to concentrate. A birdie on a par 4, in the dark and I did not lose a dime!

We broke open the best bottle of wine that the clubhouse had to offer at the ensuing dinner, and I repeat what I had said before: this was, indeed, a prestigious club.

On the way home, I once again savored the round that had begun so miserably, only to have delivered such an unsuspecting climax. I felt that the feeling was too glorious to allow it to be interrupted by the thought that this was another challenge from the golf virus to seduce me into continue playing, like a parasite that consumes a body while making sure it stays alive so that it can continue feeding on it. My first thought was that it was just luck, but was it really a coincidence that we had both played that last hole so well? I could have expected that from my buddy as he was a much better player than me, but then again, in the dark? Then the doubt came. Was it luck? If Coach had been right, then my birdie did not happen despite, but because of the dark. After all, it made absolutely no sense to look and see where the ball would land. You could barely have seen it take off, or worse yet, you could barely have seen it on the tee box. You needed all your concentration to do nothing else but... hit the ball.

-8-

On the actual day of the club competition, I left with mixed emotions and encountered a horrible flight. Yes, I know; stroke play in golf is an individual sport where you only have two opponents: the course and yourself. Yet a difficult flight could easily be the reason for aggravating circumstances. The fun thing about a stroke play competition is that you can support one another in the contest against yourself and the course, not unlike real life. You can, however, also be surrounded by people who don't contribute in any way to your round of golf, but who aren't a hindrance to you either. That's less enjoyable, but since you know it's only for a couple of hours, you think: oh well, better luck next time. Well, that is not how it is in real life.

Thirdly and lastly, you can wind up with those one-off flights from hell. These are the ones that distract you from playing your own game. These are people in flight who do not know the rules of the game and do nothing but unwittingly upset your concentration, or even worse, purposely make your life difficult because they think they are playing against you. They invented match play especially for those people. The problem being, most of them do not play it.

Well, it was my turn that day. I was the marker for someone, who, apparently unwittingly, counted incorrectly at every hole. These things happen of course, but she questioned every score I marked down. Only after I reviewed every stroke meticulously, did the woman admit she that was wrong. She did not score well because her handicap was adjusted more for her mathematical skills than her game. That is why she was angry with me.

The other man in the flight was even worse than someone who does not know the rules. He thought he knew the rules but managed to confuse them continuously. Like the time he scolded me because I had turned my marked ball on its axis to line it up, based on the winter rule that states that you may place the ball once due to adverse conditions. He was bringing up rules that only applied to pros, such as the ban on brush tees. I did not even want to be having these discussions and they were driving me mad! A marshal even intervened to bring him down a notch and to avoid me being penalized for a so-called infraction of the rules. Luckily, the marshal said I was right and apparently there were enough people around to shut the rule-buster up. He never said another word to me for the remainder of the round – and that was fine by me.

The only luck that seemed to befall me that day was that the flight was not slow. Apparently, that task was assigned to the flight ahead of us. Do you know the kind of people who have no appreciation whatsoever for their surroundings and play golf as if hitting a ball signifies a rude interruption of the conversation they are having? Well, that is how I experienced these four people ahead of me, eighteen holes long, as they refused to let us pass them by.

Despite all the commotion, I played a decent competition. Four strokes better than my handicap and second place gave me a score that had surpassed my expectations. At my request, my handicap was adjusted throughout. Could it be that crazy Coach's simple theory was for real after all? That seemed a bit farfetched to me. I will have to admit that it frequently crossed my mind during the competition. As long as I concentrated, did not get too distracted and tried to do nothing else but hit the ball, all went well, despite the numerous disruptions by my flight companions. Okay, that bit of instruction did not turn me into a super player, but I had definitely improved. This was undoubtedly true, and all that counted in this case.

-9-

While cleaning out my golf bag the following day, I found Coach's business card. I thought I would give him a call and share my accomplishments with him, but I could not get hold of him. His phone immediately switched to voicemail. The second time around I decided to leave a message. I felt a little stupid after I hung up. I was like a little kid who had to call Daddy and let him know how well he had done. Well, no harm in being proud, even for such a minor accomplishment as mine. Considering my talent, it was huge.

I received a text-message later that day on my cell phone. The message was somewhat mysterious. It read: "First Saturday of next month, 2 p.m." and then the address with the message: "He is expecting you."

I knew who the sender was: Coach. Only I did not know who was expecting me.

I thought it weird that Coach had not called or congratulated me or did not even show an interest in my accomplishment and how I had made it happen. Was he waiting for me to show some improvement beforehand? Would he take me seriously? He could have had a myriad of intentions. And why was he being so mysterious?

Was it because he did not want to instruct me himself and was trying to find a way to get rid of me? Had he found out somehow that I played for money, and was he going to turn me in? It was the first time that I became fearful of this. Then there was that silly message without any explanation. Had he really gone all out, he could have been even more cryptic, like: at the sign of the second full moon after the cleansing of the water in the grass, follow the stuttering wolf. Now that would have been mysterious! Okay, guys, this is about a simple game of golf, not the establishment of a new world order.

By coincidence, I played two more money games before that Saturday appeared on the calendar, but with little success. It did not go that badly, certainly not when I took a practice swing, but by the time I had to actually hit the ball, a hundred and one thoughts went through my mind, making sure I did the strangest things. It is unbelievable how after a while, you can stand there hacking away as if you do not really know how to swing your club anymore. It is as if your joints are fighting your muscles, which in turn cannot get along with your tendons. That bickering between the different parts of my body resulted in a cacophony not unlike an orchestra that had decided to play different scores simultaneously.

Balls were flying every which way, depending on what part of my body had the upper hand at the time of the ongoing inner battle. My score was so low I could have cried; I lost $9,000 and decided I would take revenge on my damned body. It was mostly my liver and kidneys that wound up paying in the process, even if they were in fact innocent. Oh well, isn't it always the innocent that suffer the most during times of war? I assumed that my vital organs would take it upon themselves to have a talk with the rest of my body and get all parts in sync.

The second wager was more of a mental screw-up. Because the previous round had been so terrible, I tried to play it safe and was quick to learn that is just not my style. I was always ten yards short on par 3, my bunker shots were not aggressive enough, and so I repeatedly failed to get the ball out. I flubbed the chips because I wanted to use a soft touch to drop the ball in the hole, and the putts – oh, those damned putts. Did you ever have that feeling that you are always replaying the previous putt? Of course you do. We've all been through that. You putt short and then you put too much power into your next stroke, even though you are closer to the hole. Hence you overshoot the hole. Then you putt too soft to compensate for the previous putt, etc. Consequently, your confidence sinks so low that every stroke – not only your putt – turns out wrong. Small anomalies that you would normally accept as being normal now become signs of your ignorance. After 18 holes you leave the course a mental wreck.

It was in that state of mind, and $8,000 poorer, that I went to my mysterious appointment.

-10-

The first Saturday of the following month I headed over to the address sent to me in the message. I had expected to wind up on a golf course, but after a bit of searching, I found my destination on an unpaved road in the middle of the woods where the carpet of leaves muffled the sound of the tires. It was an estate with a large, wrought-iron gate crowned with an ornate molding and a cast-iron sitting dog perched at the top. It was pretty impressive, especially because two cars could easily pass each other going through the gate. The gate was open, and I drove onto the property in between two gigantic rhododendrons. A magnificent lawn opened up behind the huge bushes and about 300 yards in the distance I saw what seemed to be a relatively unpretentious estate.

It must have been the country house or hunter's lodge of some noble family. It was not geared to long stays of pomp and circumstance, but more to a weekend away with the boys. The small house exuded an atmosphere of a long-lived-in residence, pregnant with adventure and the hunt. A plume of blue smoke emanated from the natural stone chimney, which from my perspective, barely protruded from the natural slate roof. It was a single-level house and the roof sloped almost down to the ground on the left. As you approached, you could see where the firewood was kept dry under the roof overhang. The blocks of wood looked bone dry and were neatly piled up.

I drove up to the massive oak door at the side where the roof slanted upward. I could see in the side of the wall, two tall glass doors that had most likely been built in at a later date, which, when swung open would provide unimpeded access to the gigantic garden. It was more a park than a garden with its wide lawn, surrounded by woods filled with oak and beech trees and intertwined by two brooks that fed into a pond at the outer edge of the property.

As soon as I stepped out of the car, it was apparent to me that the serenity that engulfed you in this domain was extraordinary. Even the birds seemed to respect the silence by not chirping too loudly. Now and then the cry of a magpie fell out of sync, but otherwise the birds seemed to wait patiently for their turn to sing. I wandered over to the door, but before I could knock, the oak colossus swung open. I instinctively took a step back. A man appeared out of the obscure room from behind the door. He appeared to look right through me, as if he were looking at something behind me. I instinctively turned around. He was probably sizing up my car, which I was pretty proud of myself.

"The newest model." I mumbled with a shy smile.

"Excuse me?"

"The car… newest model, six cylinders."

"Oh, that," he answered with a jovial smile on his lips. "Come in."

"Feel free to take a look," I continued. Checking a car out was always a good icebreaker. "You can take a spin in it if you like."

"Thank you, that's very kind of you, but I wouldn't advise it."

"Fine." I mumbled, confused and a little insulted.

"Come on in."

The man turned around. He was dressed in loose clothing that seemed to float around his body. It had the air of a samurai's robe, but just a tad more discreet. He was not wearing an obi. His vest was made of supple, shiny cotton with a Mao collar. He looked very elegant, but a little strange. I figured him to be about sixty years old, based on his graying, thinning and medium-length hair and the wrinkles around his eyes and mouth.

His movements, due to the flamboyant clothing, had an es-
thetic fluidity and an elegance that made me envious of him
immediately. His ballet-like shoes made his footsteps not only
light, but silent as well. I followed him, and every step I took
felt like a clumsy interruption of the harmony that seemed to
revolve around the room like a warm flow of air. I was embarrassed every time my heavy black shoes touched the ground,
and I tried to walk on tip-toe. It looked more like I had just
done a number two in my pants.

The house was pretty dim until my host walked over to the
light switch and turned on a frugal light in the corner of the
room that was the darkest. Contrary to the rustic character
of the hunter's lodge, there was a minimum of furniture. There
were some cushions for sitting, a low and a high table with
four chairs. An AGA cooker provided pleasant warmth that
felt like it had crept into the stone walls. There were no TVs or
computers to be seen. In the corner stood a well-filled, bright
yellow golf bag, with all the traditional accoutrements. Nothing
unusual at first glance.

"Coach sent me to you."

"I know. The pleasure is all mine."

I started to feel a little uncomfortable. Here I was with a complete stranger on the advice of another complete stranger. I
did not know why I was here, or what this guy's role was. For

all I knew this could wind up being a huge misunderstanding leading to an even more uncomfortable situation.

"Nice place."

"It's comfortable living here."

"Nice view too."

"Could it be that Coach neglected to tell you everything?" he asked, with the hint of a smile.

"I have to admit that I hardly know him. I only met him once."

"Then it's nice he picked you. There must have been a special reason for that."

"Yup, pity, I suppose. I'm not that talented."

"That could be," he said, without a trace of irony. "Why are you here?"

For a moment I was caught off guard by the straightforward-ness of this man, which, based on his appearance, I had not expected.

"He had the impression that I could learn something from you. As do I, of course," I quickly added, not letting him doubt my motivation.

"What is it you want to learn?"

"Golf."

"You want to learn how to hit a ball?"

I could not help but smile. "That's how you can recognize good golfers," I said.

"By what?"

"By the casual attitude they have when they talk about the game. But like I already said: I don't have that much talent. So, it's a struggle for me."

"And you hope that I have the magic formula."

"It's simply because I think that I'm doing something fundamentally wrong."

"Who doesn't? Do you think that there are people who play perfect golf? The game of golf is completely different than most other sports."

"What do you mean? Isn't Tiger Woods fabulous?"

"Fabulous is not perfect, and you might want to question whether he would rather be perfect than fabulous."

"And why is that?"

"Did Coach tell you anything about how golf differs from other sports?"

"Yes, I think he did, that golf is about not making mistakes. Is that it?"

"That's the basic principle." He nodded and showed a blissful smile.

"So, there's only one thing for me to do and that's to perfect my game," I sighed.

"Yes," he answered to my dismay. "The only question is: how?"

"That's the question I was just going to ask you, because that's quite an undertaking for someone with little talent. And quite frankly, it's frustrating. That's why I was thinking that I'm missing something." I conveniently left out the pressure caused by me playing for money and losing it at a concerning rate.

"Do you understand golf?" he asked me in a tone of voice that added some intensity to this question.

"What do you mean?"

"Do you have the impression that you understand the essence of golf?"

He had hit the nail on the head. I did indeed have the feeling that something about the basic element of the sport was eluding me. "No, I certainly don't have that feeling," I sighed.

"Good, then there's hope."

His cryptic way of speaking threw me off balance.

"It's not because the basic principle is perfection that there isn't a faster way to get there."

I did not quite get what he was saying, and so I just said something I did know. "Coach said that every mistake in golf is a mental error."

The man laughed. "That's right."

"He demonstrated that with an example."

"What example was that?"

"He showed me why I sometimes hit the ground and why at other times I topped the ball."

"And was he right?"

"I think so. I played better afterwards."

"Where did you go wrong then?"

"Still often enough; like with my approach."

"And?"

"My last shot landed for the most part on the left side of the green."

"Is that all?" he asked.

"Well, that was bad enough, but that's not all, no. I'm afraid that if we get started on my list of shortcomings, we might be at it for quite a while."

"Coach probably told you to just hit the ball."

"Yup, that's right."

"And you did that."

"Yup, and it worked, at least for a while."

"That's weird."

"Real weird. Even though I'm doing all I can to improve my game, it lately seems like I'm playing worse instead of better."

"That's weird," he repeated.

"Really weird, that's what I just said."

"What I mean is, that you're doing all you can to improve your game. What does that entail?"

"Well, I try to hit the ball more cleanly, for example."

"Oh, now I get it."

"What?"

"Why you've regressed."

"And why is that?"

"A mental error."

"Aah, you guys are driving me nuts. It's always about those mental errors. Which one is it now?"

"Simple. You want to improve on perfection."

"Perfection? Man, I'm a slob!" I lost my cool for a second

there. My outburst scarred the serenity of the surroundings. The man let my words dissipate and appeared to be looking through me. He kept on smiling.

"That could be, but apparently you were doing something right."

"Right, maybe. But not perfect."

"You need to put that into perspective. There's always an element of coincidence in perfection that you have no control over, but it's not about that now."

"Then what is it about now?" I replied impatiently.

"That you knew that you had to do nothing else but hit the ball, but that you wanted to do it in a more refined way, more elegant and cleaner."

"Oh, so that was where I was going wrong. That's where I wanted to improve on perfection, but my strokes weren't all that perfect."

"It's not about perfection of the stroke, but perfection of the thought."

I moved closer to the edge of my chair. "What do you mean?"

"If your thought is perfect, then your stroke can either be perfect or good. The results run parallel to each other."

"But if my thought is perfect, why isn't my stroke?"

"That's due to the inevitable change of coincidence. No matter how well a machine is built, anomalies, whereby a certain percentage of the machine's output is defective, are always taken into consideration. It shouldn't come as a surprise to you that this also occurs with the imperfect machine that is the human body. The trick is to not be distracted by inevitable anomalies. The greatest mistake is that people leave their perfect thoughts behind and correct a coincidental error by making a permanent correction."

"Is that such a bad thing?"

"No, only if you find it important to play good golf consistently."

I growled. Well of course, nothing is important if you do not have any ambition. Only I was not about to give up that quickly on my ambition, although I realized that it had dropped quite a bit since I started playing the game. There is a bit of Tiger Woods or Jack Nicklaus in every one of us, you know. The reality is that for the most part, we are who we are. And as far as golf was concerned, I was not liking who I was.

"So, you say that thinking a perfect swing is the most important thing."

"Yes, without a doubt."

"Does that mean there's nothing to it other than just hitting the ball?"

"That's right. The rest just pollutes your thought process, and you wind up doing all kinds of weird stuff."

"But I have been doing them for a reason."

"That reason being?"

"Well, as a matter of fact, just simply the idea that, well, you know, I can't believe it's so simple."

"You don't believe that it works, despite the fact that you've seen that it works."

"I might believe that it works; only I think it can work better."

"How so?"

He had a point there. No matter what I had tried, it only worked against me.

"But it's not because I don't know how that there's not a better way."

"And yet it's so."

"But every reasonable cell in my brain is resisting that it can be done in that manner. How can I hit the ball nicely, when I hit it as if I'm hitting it into the ground?"

"That's precisely what the essential difficulty of golf is all about. Would you like something to drink?"

"Sure, water is fine."

The man stood up. I noticed that he stood up a bit stiffly, somewhat in contrast to the elegance he had displayed when walking. He briefly groped for the handle of the refrigerator in the open kitchen. Not a very solid grip for someone involved with physical control.

My gaze wandered off to outside. I saw a red flag about 150 yards off in the distance. The immense lawn was, as far as I could see, at least one hole. Par 3 no doubt, because I saw a tee box on the right and in between the flag and the tee box was a fairway in the shape of an hourglass.

My host returned and placed a glass of water in front of me. He looked past me and only now did I notice it.

I took another good look at his eyes to be absolutely sure. "But you're blind!"

"Thank you for making me aware of that." He held that playful smile that shone all the way up to the edges of his eyes. "I can't see that myself. One of the strange twists of fate: you know it without seeing it, because if you could see it, you wouldn't know it."

I laughed sheepishly at the stupidity of my remark. "I can understand it being an annoying handicap."

"Why is that? We only call it a handicap because others can see. Would you call it a handicap that you can't read minds or move objects solely by the power of concentration?"

"No, of course not. Nobody would."

"Exactly. But theoretically, it is a handicap."

"Can you then?"

"No. What do you think?"

"But you people can do things that we can't do," I said, trying to comfort him, but actually wanting to erase my own uncomfortable feeling in a clumsy way.

"Who might you people be?"

"Geez, I'm sorry, I didn't mean it like that. You know, I just meant, like people who can't see." I realized that I was just sinking deeper into the mud as a result of my thoughtless utterances.

"No need to apologize. The fact that I'm blind doesn't mean that I automatically inherit other qualities. I have talent and skills, just as you do, but that has nothing to do with being able to see or not. Except for one thing."

"That being?"

"That being, I don't have the handicap of being able to see."

"You mean not being able to see," I corrected him.

He paused for a moment and then turned his head in my direction as if he were looking me straight in the eye.

"No, I really mean being able to see. I will never be tempted to look where I shouldn't be looking."

I shook my head in confusion.

He continued: "I asked you a while ago if you really understood golf."

"That's right, and I didn't quite understand the question," I admitted.

"To be able to play golf well, you need to have an understanding of what you're doing. The essence of golf is that it's based on actions that go against our intuition. You can overcome this intuition in two ways."

"Aha! I have a choice."

"No, not really. If you don't have the one, you're relegated to try and achieve the other."

"Okay, now you lost me. Is it my fault that I don't get it?"

The blind man laughed boyishly. "Hmm, then both options are still open."

"What do you mean?" I asked now totally confused.

"Sorry, just kidding. There are maybe just two ways to play really good golf. The first one is to be stupid enough to not think logically. The second one is to be smart enough to achieve the essence of golf."

"Aha! I once said the same thing about painting."

"What do you mean?"

"Painting, you know – landscapes and stuff like fruit. Still life." I looked straight into my host's glassy eyes. "Oops. I'm sorry.

For a moment there I forgot you were blind."

"Doesn't matter. I know what a painting is."

"Once again, my apologies. Forget what I said. I'm so rude."
I noticed I was still explaining everything using hand gestures.

"Not to worry, the conversation is more enjoyable when you're
not so considerate of me. Tell me about your theory on painters."

"Well, it's more like a joke, really. I say this primarily because
I have absolutely no talent for painting, as opposed to just
about every other member of my family."

"Tell me anyway. I'm crazy about jokes."

"Actually, now that I think about it, it's not even funny enough
to be a joke. I'm only telling you this out of self-defense."

"Okay, so what is it then?" His tone was surprisingly patient.

"Well, you know, I always say that being able to paint well is
like a freak of nature. A handicap, if you will. This is simply
because you need to be able to perceive a three-dimensional
reality in a limited manner. Good painters don't see three dimensions, but see two dimensions immediately, which they
then apply to the canvas. Similarly to what you say about golf,

you could say that you need either to be too stupid to see the three dimensions, or so smart that you can convert the three dimensions into two."

"You might have a point there," said the blind man. Despite not being able to use his eyes, you could still see a twinkle in them and they were encircled by wrinkles of joy that gave him his boyish allure despite his age.

"Come on. Let's go outside."

He stood up and I followed him, quickly slurping the last of my water. It is ironic that just when you want to avoid making any noise, you wind up slurping. My host turned and the wrinkles of joy appeared once again. He did not miss a thing… that was certain. He graciously threw open the double glass doors that led to the garden. The sounds of nature surfed inside on a wave of fresh air.

"Would you grab that bag for me?"

I lifted the golf bag that I had noticed earlier in the corner of the room. A second glance did not reveal any exceptional clubs. It contained an average mixture of iron, wood, hybrids and a relatively simple putter.

I briefly lost sight of my host and when I looked up again, he appeared from the left side of the house. I followed my newfound guru to the tee box. Only now did I notice that he had a large axe in his right hand and a saw in his left. The axe was one of those that you only see lumberjacks in checkered shirts carrying around in those documentaries about the backwoods of Canada. The saw had a large red frame in relation to the somewhat modest blade. I had no idea what to make of this. I was just hoping that the axe and saw had nothing to do with golf.

"Would you like to hit a ball?" he asked while pointing with the axe to the tee.

"Can I see you in action first?" I asked, because I was dying to see how a blind man was going to either hit a golf ball or do something with an axe and a saw.

"Everyone loves a freak show," he mumbled, somewhat cheerfully.

"That's not… what I meant."

"Doesn't really matter. I understand your curiosity. May I have the 7 iron?"

I gave him the club from the bag, stepped up to the tee and laid the club down. Slowly and focused, he straightened up. He conjured up a ball from his left hand and a tee from a crease of his kimono-like outfit. He placed both of them on the box.

He used his right hand to produce another small device from another crease. It wasn't much larger than two matchboxes back-to-back, lengthwise. He moved a button. A red led light lit up on top of it. I thought I heard a light buzzing sound. The man pressed a button that I couldn't see too well because his thumb was covering it and most of the device was covered by the rest of his hand. A tone came from the direction of the flag, artificial, but not unpleasant, clear, crisp, the auditory equivalent of a laser beam. If this device was designed to help blind people, I questioned what the purpose of the green light was. Such silly thoughts have occurred to me before.

The blind man then felt for the two wooden beams that cordon off the tee. He used his left hand to press the tee, with the ball on it, into the ground. He once again straightened himself in a flowing, almost slow-motion-like movement, and without hesitation reached for his club. He pressed anew on the button of the device. A short beep sounded from the ball. He stood perfectly still and returned the device into the crease of his kimono. He felt for the grip of his club and held it loosely.

His backswing was just as elegant as the rest of his moves. The sound that the club produced was similar to that of a sword that split the air, and after a velvet-soft tap, the ball departed with a beautiful trajectory only to land a few yards in front of the green. It bounced a yard onto the green, three yards from the flag and a bit to the left. He came off the tee box walking like a dancer, his toes touching the ground first.

"Has your curiosity been quenched?"

I stood with my mouth agape. His question interrupted a thousand thoughts of astonishment and surprise that were flashing through my mind. I shook my head in amazement.

"How do you know if it's a good lie?"

"I think so, but I can't know for sure. Is it a good lie?"

"Ready for birdie."

The man produced the device again. He pressed the left button whereby the flag sent the sound our way. He then appeared to press the other button. I heard nothing, but apparently the blind man did. It was the sound of the ball.

"Hmm, a little to the left."

"And the distance?" I asked as a senseless challenge that might have even been inappropriate.

"I would need to stand somewhere else first, but it should be about right."

"Of course, sorry 'bout that."

"No apology necessary. Now it's your turn."

All the golf instruction I have ever had or read flashed through my mind and I knew that it would all wind up in a hodgepodge that would confuse me to such an extent that I would most likely flub the shot. I gently took the 7 iron from his hands and took my stance on the tee. My clothing was not as comfortable as I would have liked and even though I was wearing sporty shoes, they were not my trusty golf shoes. In order to keep my composure, I decided in a flash of enlightenment to eradicate the chaotic thoughts from my mind and imitate the graceful posture of the blind man. If I could not find peace and quiet now, I could always pretend I had. I realized that if I wanted to be overcome by elegance and inner peace, I would have to do it myself. After all, the man was blind. What could happen? Would he be paying attention to my style, or correct my swing? How would he do that? He could at very best, listen for the impact of the club on the ball and after that go on good faith that the ball had a good lie. Or would he be giving me one of those beeping balls too?

Ridiculous. That would mean that he did not trust me. He threw me a regular ball made by well-known manufacturer. I grasped for the ball but missed it. Sigh. It had landed next to the blind man's tee that was still in the ground. I placed the ball on it. I calmly breathed in and then out and with my eyes shut, made a few gestures as if it was me wearing the kimono. I looked at the flag again, took my stance and executed my swing with the utmost concentration. The ball took flight with an astounding trajectory and landed graciously on the green. It continued to roll a bit and stopped in the fringe right behind the green, off to the left of the flag. Moments like these, for an average golfer and an outstanding slob like me, are moments when you cannot help but feel anything but proud. I just barely managed to keep myself from saying, "Did you see that?" You feel blessed when you yourself are convinced that nothing can go right and then everything goes right. My new teacher was unmoved. I said nothing. I was already too busy adopting an indifferent manner, as if this was my normal level of play.

"And?" he asked.

"Yup, beautiful."

"Do it again."

How I hated that. Why do people always have to disrupt that perfect piece of happiness by getting you to do it all over again, only to then fail and destroy every glimpse of joy with the devastating reality of the average? The blind man threw me another ball. I caught it overhand. The tee wound up about a yard behind the spot where he had placed it, on an oak leaf. It was still intact. I stuck it in the ground, just next to the hole that was left there from the previous time. I placed the new ball on the tee and took my stance. I concentrated entirely on what had just led to my perfect ball. I tried to focus on exactly imitating the movements that I had just made and in my opinion, succeeded in doing so. I could therefore hit with a little less power, seeing the distance I had just been able to attain. The direction had been satisfactory, but maybe I needed just a tad correction to the right. The result of all this contemplation however, was pathetic. The ball flew crookedly way off to the right and wound up about level with the flag, but at least 15 yards to the right and in the woods. I was extremely disillusioned, but on the other hand, this was a realistic reflection of my golfing skills.

"No good?" the man asked, probably because of the sound. If it had not been that of the hit, then it was the sound of rustling leaves in the woods that tipped him off.

I shook my head.

"You're probably shaking your head right now, but I can't see that. Was it okay?"

"Nope, sorry... slice. Slice."

It was more of a push slice, almost a shank, but I did not want to be the anatomist-pathologist of this corpse of a shot.

"Hit another one." He threw me a new ball and a tee.

I lunged at the ball, but because I wanted to catch the tee as well, I caught neither. This was not good publicity for my eye-hand coordination. I sighed at my clumsiness and bent over to tee up the ball. I took my correct stance and took another look over my shoulder at the flag.

"What are you planning to do?"

"Er, simple – I'm going to try and hit the ball as close as possible to the flag," I said, like a smartass.

"Right, there's your problem," he stated, undisturbed.

"I thought the whole idea behind the game was to hit the ball towards the flag?" I asserted my attitude.

"That's what your intuition is telling you. Didn't I mention a little while ago how on a couple of points, golf goes against your intuition?"

"On a couple of points. That would also mean that on a couple of points, it doesn't. How can I make that distinction?"

"Intuition," he said dryly.

"You're kidding, right?" I said, more confused than I wanted to appear.

"Maybe a little. But still, the difficulty and the essence of golf are about things we must do that go against our gut feeling, and even more so, things that are contrary to what we want as a result."

"What do you mean by that? Do you mean that using a piece of metal to hit a ball into a hole is an unnatural action? I could indeed believe that this isn't programmed into our genes. The survival of man didn't depend on such of folly back in pre-historic times. Maybe I need to switch to the ancient sport of mammoth hunting or something."

The blind man laughed, unperturbed. "As human beings, we are used to looking in front of us. All our actions take place before us. Our eyes are set in the front of our heads and we do all our things straight ahead of us, rarely at our sides. Most sports are geared to that. In football, tennis, bicycling, run-ning, throwing… all motions move forward. Golf is completely different. Golf is played laterally. We must execute an unusu-al movement and try to coordinate all our senses unnaturally well."

"So golf is more suitable for crabs."

"You could say that. If crabs were to invent a similar sport, they would have to move forward while playing it. Football, for instance," he continued.

"Those claws would be tough on the goalkeeper," I added unnecessarily.

"Probably. It's just as tough for us to hit or putt sideways. We even have difficulty looking sideways and that's why just lining the ball up is already the cause of many a mistake."

"And is the entire difficulty of playing golf based on this principle?"

"If only that was all there was to it. There are many other things in golf that go against our intuition, only they are much more difficult to reason out. We can safely call them the contradictions of the game of golf."

"And will I ever understand them?" I asked hesitantly, because I feared the answer.

"You mean will you ever master them?"

"Preferably."

"Shall I first explain what they are?"

"Of course, let's start with that. I think I know a few, but go ahead."

"There aren't that many, you know."

"But enough to mess up your game," I sighed.

 "Which ones do you know?"

"I could think of a few. Let's take putting, for instance. If your eyes follow where the ball is going, you'll pull it to the left. You have to force yourself not to look."

"Very good."

"And it's the same thing when you tee off."

"Okay, go ahead," he encouraged me.

"Well, if, after you tee off, you want to see how nicely the ball flies, and follow where it goes, the ball will flop off the tee right in front of your feet because you'll top it."

"Do you see the contradiction in that?" the blind man asked with a restrained giggle that made him seem almost alien.

"As a matter of fact, I do. If I hadn't looked and topped it anyway, I would've seen the ball, because I wouldn't have lost sight of it that way."

"And if you hadn't looked, then you would have had enough time to see that nice fight," he concluded.

"That's why I played so well in the dark the other day," I mused, more to myself.

"My sentiments exactly." A sad smile appeared on his face.

"I can't think of anymore right now. Are there others?" I asked, to keep the energy flowing.

"Yes. For instance, if you try to direct the ball and you're right-handed, you will either pull it left or slice it right."

"That explains why for a while after my encounter with Coach, I would hit the ball nicely until the flag came within reach…"

"Exactly!" he affirmed.

"Oh, I just thought of another one: when I'm chipping and I want to scoop the ball up, it doesn't go. For me to bring the ball up, I need to hit down on it."

"You're learning fast. There are a few more like that."

"Isn't there a list with all of them on it?" I asked, for the short-cut.

"No, but there aren't that many either. If we add that in order to keep control over your club on impact, you must be prepared to relinquish control over your club at the end of your backswing, we've covered just about all of them."

I took a moment to allow all of this to sink in. It seemed to agree with what had been my experience. But how was I supposed to apply it?

"Now you're undoubtedly asking yourself how you're going to do this."

I was startled from my contemplation. For a moment, I had the feeling that the blind man could read my thoughts. "That's right. It looks great on paper, but how can I apply it in practice?"

"You don't have to do anything with it for now. The most important thing is that you now realize that you shouldn't be trying to reason out everything."

"Okay, but sooner or later I should always be able to conjure up a beautiful swing from my sticks, preferably with some consistency."

"'Always' and 'consistently' have the same meaning."

He was right, but I did not come here for a lesson in grammar.

"Just like with everything else," the blind man continued, "we tend to want to do things twice. We believe we can think about and process different things simultaneously. This doesn't work in a practical sense. We double up on things and therefore we miss everything."

"But you're supposed to think about everything in golf. You would need a dual-core processor in your brain to analyze all the points whereby you can execute a swing incorrectly."

The blind man nodded. I wondered whether he would also have that reflexive action if he were speaking to another blind man. Another one of those silly thoughts.

"All the misery inherent in modern day amateur golf might have started with the analysis of the swing," he said. "When you split it up into all the different elements, you get a fantastic theoretical model of the swing, but it's impossible to execute it as one fluid motion."

"And yet that's the common practice. Isn't that what the pros live on?" I asked.

"Well, it works, on the condition that you spend enough time to improve on every aspect that you're doing wrong and that you practice until it seems as if it were ingrained in the memory of your muscles."

"Boy, that's tiresome. But I guess one doesn't have much choice," I stated fatalistically.

"Come here for a bit." He made a gesture that pointed at the axe that was leaning up against the tree.

"Do you want me to take the axe?" I asked.

"Yes, please."

I laid my club on the ground, took a few steps forward on the left and behind the blind man and hesitatingly grabbed the heavy axe.

"If I'm not mistaken, there should be a tree to my left that has been sawn down to less than 7 feet."

I did indeed see what must have been a pine tree or something similar. I am no botany specialist and continuously confuse pine trees with spruce firs. The tree was dwarfed by the majestic oak and beech trees. That is probably why it had been sawn down. The stump was just a little bit larger than me and was still firmly rooted in the ground. Resin had overflowed from where the tree had been cut, which gave the rough bark the appearance of a dripping candle. When I was a child, a similar sight would have made it hard for me to resist making torches by dipping branches in the half-congealed resin and setting them on fire.

"Take a relaxed whack at the tree," he ordered, in a monotonous voice.

"On top or on the side?"

"As if you want to chop it down."

For a moment I had the feeling that I was doing a take for the Karate Kid. It wouldn't be long now and I would be playing golf based on some wax-on wax-off principle. I even doubted whether I wanted to continue with this. I looked hesitatingly at the axe, the tree and the blind man and peeked to see if there were any spectators or maybe a hidden camera.

"Go ahead," the man encouraged me.

I hesitated once more, grabbed hold of the axe and with a huge swing, planted it in the tree. I felt the shudder of the impact from my hands to my elbows and over my biceps up into my shoulders. A small white sliver of wood had jumped out of the axe cut in the tree and landed in the blind man's grey hair. He plucked it from his scalp with his right hand and turned his head in my direction.

"Excellent!" he said.

"How do you know?"

"Nobody does that wrong."

"Well, if nobody does that wrong, why am I doing it?"

"To prove to you that you have talent, just like everyone else."

"That's good to know if I ever have to compete in a wood-chopping championship. Does this mean that you're giving up on me with regard to golf?" I said, nonchalantly.

"No, on the contrary. I wanted to show you that everyone has the skills to swing an axe into a tree. This, in fact, is a natural movement and we don't need a single pro to help us with this. Apparently, the problem arises when we take that exact motion and start calling it golf. It then becomes more complicated and we start undertaking all kinds of maneuvers. And why is that? Is it because of the ball?"

"But there is a difference: we have to hit that ball somewhere. My motion ends in the tree with the axe."

"Aha! And now we've arrived at the core of the problem."

"And that is?" I leaned on the axe in the tree like a real cool guy anticipating the revealing of the secret.

"You want to hit a ball away, towards the hole."

"That seems logical to me," I replied, disappointed. Annoyed, even.

"And that's why I've already told you that golf is not logical."

The smile that appeared on his face seemed to be a mirror image of the frown on my forehead. "Where did you put my golf bag?"

"It's off to your right, in front of the tee area."

The blind man carefully moved over and found the bag by feeling for it. He felt the club heads and removed one. "Take this one," he said.

I walked over to him and took the club. It was a different 7 iron. This one had a metal shaft. I stepped onto the tee area and wanted to prepare my shot when the golf guru just managed to grab my arm.

"Not necessary, not yet. Go back to the tree," he commanded.

"The one with the axe?"

"Yes, that one."

Not understanding, I walked over to the resin-covered stump.

"Now execute the exact same stroke with the club as you did with the axe."

"What do you mean?"

"Just do as I say. Act as if you're going to hack into the tree with the axe, but do it with the club."

"You want me to destroy your club?"

"That's right," he assured me.

"Are you sure?"

"It's only a club."

"Do you want me to remove the axe first?"

"That would seem like a safe thing to do." He talked to me as if I was an adolescent.

I laid the club on the ground in front of me, stepped over it and used both hands to wrest the axe from the tree that had once either been a pine tree or spruce fir. I also noticed the saw from the corner of my eye and was wondering what kind of lesson that was going to entail. I planted the axe in a trunk off to the right and behind me. It occurred to me that this might have been the victim of a previous lesson. I took the club with the iron shaft and prepared to hit the tree trunk. The blind man had moved over and now stood behind me.

"I'm not going to get the clubhead on my head, am I?"

"Just swing and make sure the head of the club hits the trunk solidly, just like you did with the axe."

The club whizzed with a big yet controlled swing towards the trunk. As I anticipated, the metal shaft broke about a third of the way up from the club head. The anticipation of the break could not save me from an instinctive shock reaction, which made me duck. From the corner of my eye, I saw the him standing unmoved. Although the broken piece of club was not a threat to him, I thought it would have been polite to have yelled "FORE!"

"That sounded good," he said. "How did it feel?"

"Weird! I'm not in the habit of smashing clubs on tree trunks."

"But did you feel the swing?"

I thought for a moment about what had happened. "Well, yes, it felt like a natural and controlled swing, one where I definitely had a feel for the head of the club. The motion of all the parts of my body felt as if they were flowing into one another."

"Great, even though I want to point out that you don't really have parts in your body. You make it unnecessarily complicated once you start to think that way. Just like you shouldn't perceive the swing as being made up entirely of small positions and motions, you should also refrain from perceiving your body as a puzzle that is linked together with tendons and joints. You can't process the components if you think of them as pieces, but you can execute a motion in its entirety if you have one swing thought.

"It's similar as to how you can't describe exactly what you're doing when walking the stairs or riding a bicycle, but, amazingly enough, you manage to do it time and time again.

"And it only becomes more difficult the more you start to analyze it. Just think about being ever so careful not to trip at that important meeting. Suddenly, the possibility of tripping on the stairs becomes significantly greater."

The man was right. You could not confuse people more by asking them to explain exactly how to execute their swing. Well, maybe one way: by asking them to explain exactly how they execute a particular part of their swing, like the position of their wrists during the backswing. I can guarantee that it will go wrong then. Not surprising that things like this are not permitted in the regulations.

The blind man took a breath as if to say something and I stirred from my thoughts. "Do you think you can repeat that swing when hitting a golf ball?"

"There is a difference though, because I executed a horizontal swing and I would need to swing vertically when hitting a ball."

"The principle is the same, only with tilted hips. What I wanted to show you was that everyone has the natural ability to achieve the right stroke. Golf is more a question of finding that stroke again every time instead of developing it. All of us have the ability to do it, but we've unlearned it."

"So, what's the secret?"

"We touched on it briefly a few minutes ago, when we were talking about the difference between swinging the axe and hitting the ball with the club."

"So, it's the difference between the horizontal and the vertical swing?"

"No, that's less relevant, and by then you'd already hit the tree with your club. Before that."

"I'm sorry, I just don't know anymore. Several thoughts run through my head at once. On the one hand, your illogical reasoning seems so logical and on the other hand it's hard to believe that everything you're saying is really true."

The man laughed agreeably and said nothing, patiently waiting.

"Oh, now I remember. The difference was that I was hitting the tree trunk with the axe and with the club, but I wanted to hit the ball away."

"Exactly. Very good. So, if you just stop doing that, you'll have it."

"But I have to hit the ball away. It really does have to go to-wards, or preferably, into the hole."

"As you wish, but you won't succeed. A second thing: what were you thinking when you planted the axe into the tree?"

"Uh… nothing. As long as I hit the tree."

"So it never crossed your mind to chop it into little bits and to throw them into a fireplace?"

"Of course not!"

He nodded and waited. I did not quite get what he was say-ing. "And you wanted to hit the tree with…?" he continued.

"The head of the axe." I continued to provide the most logical answer.

"Why?"

"Well, that's what does the work."

"Exactly. And that's exactly how you should let the head of the club do its work. Just like the axe pulls at you while you swing it, so you have to let the head of the club go its own way and not fight it."

"I'm certainly willing to give it a try, but don't they say that someone is just 'hacking away' when they're playing poorly?"

"That's correct, but it's also an improper use of the English language. When we hack with an axe, it's not us that are doing the 'hacking', but the axe. If, as a golfer, you're hacking away at something, you're bringing your arms close together and you're hitting instead of swinging as you do with an axe."

He took a deep breath and continued: "First try hitting the ball as if you were hitting a tree, and then watch what happens."

"What should I do with the broken club?"

"Just throw it in the bag. I'll clean up later."

"Can I replace it for you?"

"Don't be silly. I asked you to smash it, didn't I? Why don't you try and hit the ball first?"

The broken club fell to the bottom of the bag and made a muffled sound. I stuck the head of the club in one of the side pockets with an open zipper. I turned around, stepped up to the tee area and picked up the club I had left behind. I took my stance.

"Remember: like a lumberjack who trusts his axe."

I used my utmost concentration to think about the motion of the axe as it planted itself in the wood. I even caught myself shutting my eyes during the backswing, only to open them again just before my club hit the ball. The stroke was perfect. I relished the moment while my breath escaped through my nose from my lungs, in a way that left me completely relaxed and in balance. I was slow to look up but saw how the ball completed a perfect trajectory, landing behind the flag and then ever so slowly, rolling backwards a yard or so and right up to the pin. I had never, ever experienced this much ball control before. I could not wait to prolong my enjoyment by finishing the hole, which most assuredly meant dropping a birdie and then hitting a second, maybe a third and even a fourth ball.

"Come, let's go inside," he said.

It seemed childish to protest, but the extenuating circumstances were such that I was happy like a kid in a candy shop. Still, I did not protest. I looked at the blind golf instructor, then at my ball lying invitingly on the green, then at my club and finally at the golf bag. I sighed deeply but realized that I could not take up much more of the blind instructor's time. I already felt extremely privileged to have been able to tap a bit into such knowledge from his vat of wisdom, even if I had the impression that I had not yet grasped the full meaning and scope of what he had shared with me.

My impatience got the better of me. "Is this it, then? That I should hit the ball as if I'm swinging an axe?"

The blind man stopped and turned around. The look on his face kept me mesmerized. It was somewhere between amazement and concern and I was held captive by that weird lifeless glance with the slight glimmering. "I'm afraid that it might have seemed strange if we called it that," he said, seemingly more to himself than to me. He retraced his steps until he stood right in front of me. I felt a bit uneasy because his empty eyes seemed to look right through me. I involuntarily still tried to find some sign of life in his pupils.

"The axe was nothing but a tool to make something clear to you. Grab the bag and walk with me. I'll walk you to your car."

I was now entirely certain that he thought I was an idiot, and rightly so. Maybe he just wanted me to leave on a high note because of that last stroke. Maybe he was just protecting me to prevent me from ruining the moment. I turned around and picked up the golf bag.

"Should I bring the axe?"

"No, I'll need it later on."

"Oh, another student?"

"No, I'm going to chop some wood."

"Oh, like that." There was nothing wrong with my question, but somehow I felt really stupid all over again. I had to think of something quickly to break the silence. "I think the picture is pretty clear to me now, but it can't be that simple, can it? And if it's not the way of the axe, then which way is it, essentially?"

"Essentially, it all boils down to this. You want your ball to do three things. You want a nice trajectory with sufficient height, going in the right direction, and you want the ball to land at the right distance. Correct?"

"Yup, that's right."

"How do you do that?"

"Instinctively, I would say, by hitting the ball in the right direction with the right amount of power and nicely under the ball."

"And that's where everything goes wrong. You're trying to manipulate the ball and that's impossible. When you planted the axe in the tree trunk, I asked you if you had any intention of chopping the tree down into little bits and throwing them into a fireplace. You said, of course, that wasn't your intention."

"That's right," I confirmed.

"But when we hit a golf ball, that's exactly what we all want to do. Try and compare this to someone playing pool. The player also wants his ball to hit another ball first so this one gets into the pocket, then bounce off the cushion at just the right angle only then to come to rest at a designated spot on the table."

"Correct."

"How does he do that?"

"By hitting the ball with his cue using the right angle and the right speed," I said.

"Exactly. Every motion the pool ball is going to make is already in the shot. You can't expect that the ball is going to behave differently in the various phases of the trajectory. You could be hoping for that, but that's precisely the characteristic of a poor pool player," he explained, as if he was speaking to himself.

"Good to know, next time I play pool."

"Now why would it be any different for golf? You can't manipulate the ball."

"Maybe not, but my tee-off should be such that I can make the ball fly the right distance with a nice trajectory and in the right direction."

"That's true, but how do those three elements come about?"

"Do I have to answer that?" I asked to avoid making myself look like a fool again.

"Allow me..." he said, saving me. This was probably not his intention, but I felt it was a reaffirmation of my ignorance. There was a fine line between inspiration and insecurity in my world today. "The direction that the ball takes depends on your stance and your grip."

"That's right."

"Okay, and the height and the trajectory of the ball depend on the loft of your club."

"But it also depends on the position you lay your ball and whether you open your club, right?"

"That's true," he said patiently, "but we're talking about your swing in general here, not about the tricks and exceptions you want to bring into the game."

"Yes, of course. You're right."

"What then remains is the distance. The speed of the swing being equal, this depends on the choice of club. Are you still with me?"

"Then the conclusion is simple."

"Yup, clear as a bell." I did not have a clue.

We had arrived at the house in the meantime. I set the golf bag down close to the open terrace doors but continued to eye the blind man curiously and avoided saying anything that might suggest that I would be willing to take a guess at that conclusion. Just to be sure, I dawdled a bit more with the golf bag and gave it one last twist before putting it down.

He turned to me briefly and then continued further on in the direction of my car. It took a couple of brisk steps to catch up with him.

"Like I just said, the conclusion is simple: once you've chosen the right club with the right loft, you're holding it right and you've properly lined up both your target and the ball. You can only do one more thing…"

"Hit the ball!"

"Exactly… and that's something entirely different than trying to hit the ball away towards the target. Because if all you want to do is swing at the ball and let the head of the club do the work, then you're probably automatically doing most of the other things right."

"You think so?" I asked.

"I know so. In any case, this way the action is in front of you and not sideways. So your motion is natural. Always keep the action in front of you."

"You've got a point there," I realized.

"But that's not all there is. For instance, let's look at the tip that says you should look at the spot of the ball as long as you can."

"That's tough, I find."

"It doesn't have to be. If your only goal is to hit the ball, then that tip is of no use to you. Why would you be looking any-where else if your only objective is to hit that ball in front of you? Not to send it somewhere?"

"I think I get it through and through now," I whispered.

"You might get it, but it won't always work."

"Well, that's a shame. Why not?" Just when I was feeling confident again, I feared he would crush it again. This man was golf personified.

"I've already discussed the natural anomalies with you. Don't be fooled by them. The greatest danger lies in wanting to do it all more beautifully, better and refined. That's when you'll start to regress."

I nodded understandingly, as these were practically my own words.

"And the saw, what's that for?"

The man frowned quizzically. "You mean the saw we took along with the axe? Oh, that's to saw wood with, of course." He seemed almost irritated by my stupidity. Finally.

"I thought you might have a trick up your sleeve."

He laughed condescendingly. "Not everything is about golf, Bogey."

"Thanks." I smiled and got into my car. "How much do I owe you?"

"How much do you think it was worth?"

"If it works? Priceless."

"Let's keep it at that then."

I shook the man's hand and closed the car door. I wanted to wave as I was driving off but realized that it would have been a pointless effort and besides, as I looked in my rearview mirror, I noticed that the blind man seemed to have gone with the wind.

EPILOG

One week after my encounter with the blind man, I played my buddies for $1,000 a man a hole, everybody against everybody, in a flight of four. Lady Luck was not with me that day. I missed a putt here and there and at a few crucial moments my natural anomaly started playing tricks on me, landing me in the woods and in a pond. Nevertheless, I walked into the clubhouse with four birdies, a new nickname and $30,000 richer. Luckily enough, I was playing against people I knew. A competition organized by a broker would certainly have resulted in a disqualification for that match or worse and I could even have been suspended, or worse.

I had experienced my first moment of real glory, and because my golf buddies had already won more than enough money from me, they accepted their losses on that day. Naturally, I was subjected to several below-the-belt sneers, besides the compliments and congrats, but no matter what they said, they all wanted to know my secret. I stood around smiling somewhat mysteriously for quite some time – some may have described it as silly – until I had enough booze in me to let my chuckle joke overflow into an enthusiastic story. I told them how simple it was, the whole, almost spiritual, experience, in the words of the blind golf guru. It told them about the axe; about simply hitting the ball, the grip, the stance, the position of the club, about keeping the action in front of you. With the authority of a winner, I described in detail what the blind pro had taught me and when I was done, a deep silence descended on all those present.

"Okay, if you don't want to tell us your real secret, that's okay too." And they ordered another round.

To be continued...